HOW TO BREAK SPELLS WE PLACE ON OURSELVES

HOW TO BREAK SPELLS WE PLACE ON OURSELVES

Using Shamanism and Psychology to free our minds.

THE GRAND PATH

BOOK I

HAWK SUNFIRE

Published by Spines
ISBN 979-8-89691-206-4

CONTENTS

I was writing the word "belief" when I noticed something interesting: it contains the word "lie" right in the middle. As I stared at it, thoughts began to form. While some beliefs lie in truth, others could qualify as "lies we tell ourselves." Not all lies are harmful; some are illusions our minds use to maintain their current reality, keeping us nestled within our comfort zones for a safe and manageable existence. While this is a useful strategy for survival, it doesn't serve us when it comes to growth.

Being a conscious creator involves discerning which beliefs are useful, which are not, and which are worth discarding. What we choose to carry or release shapes and determines the quality of our personal reality.

I've had the privilege of working alongside thousands of people in business and hundreds in a teacher-student setting, and what I've observed is fascinating. For some, a single concept can spark transformation — they run with it, making it work effortlessly. For others, no matter how many metaphors, analogies, or different lenses I provide, it seems they either "can't" or "won't" move forward.

The good news is that all situations are workable; the bad news is that it can slow down growth and evolution to a near standstill. While a standstill can sometimes be an organic part of the life process, it can also be a sign of self-sabotage or "FOFO" (the Fear of Finding Out) what they are truly capable of. I'm happy to offer guidance, provide solutions, and wait patiently for a student to break through at the "perfect" time (whether that's in days or weeks), but it's often frustrating for them. In some cases, it can be downright discouraging, leading to a sense of defeat.

Helping others overcome this frustration is my motivation for writing this eBook. I'm passionate about helping people break through the invisible barriers they create for themselves.

I faced significant challenges starting at a young age, which led me to wrestle with childhood PTSD as an adult. Through many lessons, I grew into a creative and resilient problem solver. My life has taken many forms: as a traveling snowboard instructor at age 19, a graphic designer at 23 (the same year I discovered I was going to be a father), and a teacher of metaphysics at 33. For the past 12 years, I've guided others in Shamanic ceremonies and earth-sourced medicines. Today, at 46, the most challenging and rewarding leg of my journey is as a conscious co-parent. These experiences have forced me to confront and release more limiting beliefs than I ever imagined. If I had held onto my limiting beliefs, I might have never left home or discovered what I was truly capable of.

Snowboarding requires us to face fears head-on, test physical limits, cope with danger and avoid death on a daily basis. Running a business demands infinite problem-solving and a mindset of possibility. Teaching metaphysics invites us to question the nature of reality and expand our minds continually. A

Shamanic journey takes us to a place where limits dissolve. Parenting, the most precious endeavor, involves discerning which beliefs we model and which we pass on, both of which shape our children's reality. When we release limiting beliefs, all these roles can be navigated with greater ease and flow.

If there's one lesson I've learned from these life experiences, it's this: when we feel stuck, the first place to look is at the limiting beliefs we might still be holding onto.

Through this book, I aim to provide you with insights and practical tools to help you identify and release your own limiting beliefs. Together, we can break free from the lies we tell ourselves and embrace a life of growth, fulfillment, and success.

With love, Hawk Sunfire

A MINDFUL APPROACH

While snowboarding, three philosophies were made clear to me. When riding through trees, I had to learn to focus on the path forward, not on the trees. If I looked at a tree, I hit that tree. If I focused on the path, I stayed on the path. This is a fitting metaphor for how to navigate the mind. When I was an instructor, I taught kids, "Where we look is where we go." If we look across or down the hill, we go that way. If we look at our feet, we fall down; it's that simple. If we are met with challenges in life, it serves to acknowledge them but don't stare at them. Look for the path through them, follow it, and it will take you where you want to go.

Another lesson was having the proper approach to a jump. When I was first starting to hit jumps, I learned that if I leaned too far in any direction (forward, back, toe edge, heel edge), it tended to end in disaster. I had to imagine a crosshair in the middle of my board between my feet and keep my energy in the middle of it. This is a metaphor for bias. If we come into any lesson with preconceived notions, leaning in one direction or another, we are not open to new information. The third lesson was "death is never far away." Meaning life is too short to live in the past, limiting, binding beliefs. With that, I challenge you to look for the path, not at the trees, and to approach this book from a neutral space.

A SIMPLE EYE TEST (OR IS IT?)

The Eye Test: Can You Spot the "F"s?

Take a moment to read the sentences below carefully. Your task is simple: count the number of times the letter "F" appears in the text.

Finished files are the result of years of scientific study combined with years of experience. Achieving the goals of any project often requires layers of unseen dedication and perseverance.

How many "F"s did you find? Pause and double-check before moving on.

The Lesson: Shifting our vision from "looking" to "seeing"

This exercise serves as a powerful reminder of how our minds filter information without us even realizing it. Often, we overlook what's right in front of us because our brains take shortcuts, skipping over familiar patterns. This same tendency applies to our beliefs—we may accept them without question, never noticing the ones that are quietly shaping our reality.

In Shamanic teachings, there is a concept known as "Shamanic sight," which goes beyond ordinary seeing. While the average person perceives only what they expect, Shamanic sight involves a deeper level of awareness. It is an acknowledgment that what we perceive is just a fraction of the whole truth. The wise one knows they don't know everything and remains open to the unknown, seeing possibilities where others may only see limitations.

These overlooked perceptions are often referred to as "scotomas"—blind spots in our awareness that obscure the full picture. In the context of limiting beliefs, scotomas can prevent us from seeing new horizons and possibilities for growth. They act like a veil, hiding opportunities and keeping us locked in familiar yet unfulfilling patterns.

This book is designed to help you uncover and overcome

these blind spots. By learning to question your assumptions and expand your awareness, you'll begin to see beyond the surface of your beliefs. You'll gain the tools to identify and release the scotomas that have limited your vision, allowing you to embrace new perspectives, deeper clarity, and the boundless potential that awaits beyond the familiar.

Just as you may have missed some of the "F"s in the exercise, there may be hidden beliefs you've overlooked. By practicing Shamanic sightseeing with an open heart and a willingness to explore the unknown—you can unveil these blind spots and step into a new way of being, where limitless possibilities and new horizons come into view. Answer: The number of "f" in the statement is ten.

THE COOKIE THEIF, BY VALERIE COX

A woman was waiting at an airport one night,
With several long hours before her flight.
She hunted for a book in the airport shop,
Bought a bag of cookies and found a place to drop.

She was engrossed in her book but happened to see,
That the man beside her, as bold as could be,
Grabbed a cookie or two from the bag in between,
Which she tried to ignore to avoid a scene.

She munched on the cookies and watched the clock,
As the bold cookie thief diminished her stock.
She was getting more irritated as the minutes ticked by,
Thinking, "If I weren't so nice, I'd give him a black eye!"

With each cookie she took, he took one, too.
When only one was left, she wondered what he'd do.

With a smile on his face and a nervous laugh,
He took the last cookie and broke it in half.

He offered her half as he ate the other.
She snatched it from him and thought, "Oh brother,
This guy has some nerve, and he's also quite rude.
Why, he didn't even show any gratitude!"

She had never known when she'd been so galled,
And she sighed with relief when her flight was called.
She gathered her belongings and headed to the gate,
Refusing to look back at the thieving ingrate.

She boarded the plane and sank into her seat,
Then, she sought her book, which was almost complete.
As she reached into her bag, she gasped with surprise,
There was her bag of cookies in front of her eyes!

"If mine are here," she moaned in despair,
"Then the others were his, and he tried to share."
Too late to apologize, she realized with grief,
That she was the rude one, the ingrate, the thief.

Takeaways

This story invites us to reflect on the power of our perceptions. How often do we assume we know the truth, only to find that we were wrong? The woman's frustration and judgment came from a place of misunderstanding, built upon her unquestioned belief that the cookies were hers.

We all carry assumptions and beliefs shaped by our past experiences, but this poem reminds us to pause and question them.

In moments of frustration or judgment, what if we asked ourselves:

Could I be missing something?

Could there be another story here, one I haven't considered?

Do I have the "whole" truth, or just my own?

The path to releasing limiting beliefs often begins with humility—with recognizing that our view of the world is only one perspective.

By softening our grip on what we believe to be true, we create space for new insights and a deeper understanding.

~

THE STORY OF "GRANDMA'S HAM"

In many families, traditions are passed down through generations and cherished as part of the family's heritage. But what happens when a tradition, once rooted in practicality, turns into a limiting belief that no one questions?

Consider the story of a young woman who was preparing a holiday meal. As she got ready to place a large ham in the pan, she cut off the ends before putting it in the oven. Her daughter, watching curiously, asked, "Mom, why do you cut off the ends of the ham?"

The mother hesitated. "I'm not sure," she admitted. "That's just how my mom always did it."

Wanting to find the answer, they called the grandmother. She, too, was unsure but explained, "I always cut the ends off because my mother did it. I thought it might help the ham cook better."

Still unsatisfied, they decided to ask the great-grandmother, who was now quite elderly. She chuckled when she heard the question. "Oh, that's simple," she said. "I cut the ends off because my baking pan was too small to fit the whole ham!"

What began as a practical solution for a specific situation had become a family tradition, passed down without question for generations.

~

Takeaways
This story illustrates how easily we can inherit beliefs and practices that once served a purpose but no longer fit our lives. It's a reminder to examine our beliefs, question their origins, and release those that no longer serve us. In doing so, we free ourselves from outdated traditions and open the door to new possibilities.

~

THE ROGER BANNISTER EFFECT

The story goes that running a four-minute mile was considered impossible until Roger Bannister crushed the four-minute mile mark on May 6, 1954. This gave other runners permission to question what was possible. Over the next two years, ten more athletes followed suit and accomplished the same feat, all because they were no longer held back by a psychological barrier. Chances are they were already physically able to do so, but their minds disagreed, so it was the same as not being able to do it at all.

The underlying lesson here is the power of belief and mindset in shaping our reality. The story of Roger Bannister breaking the four-minute mile demonstrates that perceived limitations are often mental rather than physical. Once the psychological barrier was shattered, others followed suit, proving that what we believe to be possible directly influences what we can achieve.

Takeaways:

Perception Shapes Reality: Our minds can act as barriers or catalysts. If we believe something is impossible, we unconsciously limit ourselves, even if the ability is already within us.

Breaking Mental Barriers: When we challenge and overcome limiting beliefs, we pave the way for personal growth and inspire others to do the same.

The Ripple Effect of Courage: Bannister's success wasn't just personal; it created a collective shift, encouraging others to reevaluate their potential.

End Results Start Within: To achieve extraordinary results; we must first let go of the mental "shackles" and embrace a mindset that sees obstacles as challenges rather than roadblocks.

When we release self-imposed limits, we unlock our true potential, transforming both our capabilities and our outcomes.

What can occur if we release the shackles on our minds?

Our end results - begin with us.

WHAT IF YOU WOKE UP TOMORROW MORNING AND REALIZED NOTHING WAS STANDING IN THE WAY OF YOUR BEST LIFE?

The obvious answers might be:

"Relieved!"
"Excited!"
"Happy!"

B ut the not-so-obvious answer is:

"Afraid of the success that will follow."

This often-overlooked fear is known as FOFO—the Fear of Finding Out. It's the subtle yet powerful hesitation to uncover your potential because, deep down, you may feel unprepared to handle the changes, challenges, or even the abundance that success can bring.

**But here's the thing:
What if you leaned into the fear
instead of running from it?**

Maybe we take one single (bold) step today to break through that invisible barrier. Write down one thing you've been holding back on—a goal, a dream, a challenge you've avoided. Then, commit to taking action, no matter how small, toward making it a reality.

Your best life is waiting for you on the other side of fear.

**The question is,
are you ready to find out what's truly possible?**

WHY IS THIS JOURNEY IMPORTANT? "BREAKING THE SPELL OF LIMITING BELIEFS"

While many of us grapple with the fear of failure, there's another, quieter foe that some battle: the fear of success, often referred to as FOFO—the Fear of Finding Out. It's the subtle apprehension that success might demand more of us than we think we're capable of giving.

More often than not, the barriers we perceive are smaller than we imagine. The operative word here is "imagine." Our thoughts, especially limiting beliefs, are often where we become trapped.

The Nature of Limiting Beliefs

Limiting beliefs can manifest as:

- Computer Viruses: Bad code disrupting our natural flow and function.
- Parasites: Draining our energy without offering anything in return except shattered dreams and self-doubt.
- Chains: Restricting our movement, keeping us confined to familiar comfort zones.
- Spells: Controlling our decisions and actions, even when they defy logic and hinder our growth.

Who Creates and Sustains these Limitations?

Accountability reveals a simple truth: we do.

It is within our rights to hold on to these beliefs—no external force forbids it. But in choosing to defend them, we also grant them control over our lives.

Our perspective is powerful. It shapes our reality. Whatever we seek, we will find. If we look for barriers, they will appear. If we seek solutions, they will reveal themselves.

A New Perspective The first step toward freedom is to identify and challenge what holds us back. When we shift from a mindset of "right and wrong" to one of "what is working or not working," we open ourselves to new possibilities.

Embracing Success with Love Growth requires courage—a willingness to challenge our comfort zones with love and compassion. By doing so, we can transcend our limitations and embrace the success waiting for us.

Wayne Dyer recounted an interaction where a woman asked him, "What are the blocks to my happiness?"

He responded, "The belief that you have blocks."

Perceived obstacles to happiness are often self-imposed beliefs. By letting go of the notion that such blocks exist, one can open the path to genuine happiness.

TAKE A MOMENT TO REFLECT:

What limiting belief has held you back the most?

What would happen if you stopped defending it?

____

____

____

____

____

____

____

____

____

____

____

____

Write it down, challenge it, and begin the process of rewriting the story you tell yourself. The first step toward success is simply this: to believe that you are worthy of it.

**Your transformation begins when
you decide to release the chains.
What's your first step?**

UNDERSTANDING THE MIND: TEN COMMON COGNITIVE DISTORTIONS

Below are some of the most common cognitive distortions, their harmful effects, and how they may show up in everyday life:

1. Disqualifying the Positive

Rejecting positive experiences by insisting they "don't count."

- **Example:** You get praised for a project at work but think, "They're just being nice."
- **Harmful Effects:** Prevents joy and satisfaction, reinforcing negativity and low self-esteem.

Reflect:
When have you been disqualifying yourself?

2. Overgeneralization

Drawing sweeping conclusions from a single event or limited evidence.

- **Example:** You make a mistake and think, "I always mess things up."
- **Harmful Effects:** Leads to unnecessary pessimism, making setbacks feel like permanent failures.

Reflect:
When have you been overgeneralizing?

~

____

____

____

____

____

____

____

____

____

____

____

____

3. All-or-Nothing Thinking (Black-and-White Thinking):

Seeing situations in extremes, such as "success" or "failure," with no middle ground.

- **Example:** You aim to exercise daily but miss one day and think, "I've completely failed my fitness goals."
- **Harmful Effects:** Discourages balanced thinking and fuels perfectionism or self-sabotage.

Reflect:
When have you been thinking in black and white?

4. Jumping to Conclusions:

Making assumptions without evidence, including:

- **Mind Reading:** "They must think I'm incompetent."
- **Fortune-Telling:** "I just know this will go wrong."
- **Harmful Effects:** Creates unnecessary anxiety and prevents positive interactions.

Reflect:
When have you been jumping to conclusions?

~

5. Catastrophizing:

Expecting the worst-case scenario, even when it's unlikely.

- **Example:** You're late to a meeting and think, "I'll get fired for this."
- **Harmful Effects:** Increases stress and often leads to avoidance behaviors.

Reflect:
When have you been catastrophizing?

6. Emotional Reasoning:

Believing your emotions reflect reality.

- **Example:** "I feel like a failure, so I must be one."
- **Harmful Effects:** Reinforces negative self-perceptions and hinders rational thinking.

Reflect:
When have you been emotionally reasoning?

7. "Should" Statements

Using rigid standards like "should," "must," or "ought" for yourself or others.

- **Example:** "I should have done better on that exam."
- **Harmful Effects:** Creates guilt, frustration, and resentment when expectations aren't met.

Reflect:
When have you been using rigid statements?

～

8. Labeling and Mislabeling

Assigning harsh labels to yourself or others based on isolated behaviors.

- **Example:** After a single mistake, you think, "I'm such a failure."
- **Harmful Effects:** Damages self-esteem and oversimplifies the complexity of human behavior.

Reflect:
When have you been mislabeling yourself or others?

~

. Personalization

Taking the blame for events outside your control.

- **Example:** A friend is upset, and you think, "It must be my fault."
- **Harmful Effects:** Causes unnecessary guilt and feelings of inadequacy.

Reflect:
When have you been personalizing events?

~

10. "They Not I" Thinking

Using biased logic in comparisons:

- "They deserved that success, but I don't."
- "They must have done something wrong, but I didn't deserve this bad outcome."
- **Harmful Effects:** Reinforces apathy, victimhood, and feelings of unworthiness.

Reflect: When have you been using biased logic in comparison?

~

STRATEGIES TO OVERCOME COGNITIVE DISTORTIONS

Recognizing cognitive distortions is the first step. Here are practical tools to help you reframe and challenge these thoughts:

1. Practice Mindfulness

Observe your thoughts without judgment. Awareness creates space for change.

2. Challenge Your Thoughts

Ask questions like:

- "What evidence supports this thought?"
- "What would I say to a friend thinking this way?"

3. Reframe the Narrative

Replace negative thoughts with balanced, constructive alternatives.

- **Example:** Instead of "I'm a failure," think, "This was one mistake. I can learn from it and do better."

4. Use Positive Affirmations

Reinforce empowering beliefs, like: "I am capable of overcoming challenges."

5. Seek Guidance

Working with a therapist, coach, or healer can provide valuable insights and support.

SELF-REFLECTION EXERCISE

Take a moment to reflect:

1 .- What cognitive distortion do you notice most often in your thinking?

2 .- How has it impacted your emotions, actions, or relationships?

3 .- What's one step you can take today to challenge this thought?

ADDITIONAL TOOLS FOR
PERSONAL GROWTH

- **The Four Agreements by Don Miguel Ruiz:**
  Offers a framework for healthier thinking.
- **Soul Root Alchemy:** A transformative process for
  releasing limiting beliefs.
- **CBT and DBT:** Evidence-based therapies that help
  reframe negative thought patterns.

Cognitive distortions can feel overwhelming, but they are not insurmountable. When you recognize and challenge these thought patterns, you regain control over your mind and life. Remember: Your thoughts shape your reality. Choose them wisely.

EXAMPLES OF LIMITING BELIEFS ABOUT MONEY

Common limiting beliefs around money can significantly impact financial well-being and personal growth. These beliefs often stem from upbringing, societal influences, and personal experiences. Here are some prevalent limiting beliefs about money:

1. "Money is the Root of All Evil"

- Origin: Misinterpretation of the biblical saying, "The love of money is the root of all evil."
- Impact: Creates a negative association with wealth, leading to guilt or discomfort in acquiring or spending money.

2. "I Don't Deserve to Be Wealthy"

   - Origin: Low self-esteem or internalized beliefs from upbringing.
   - Impact: Sabotages efforts to achieve financial success and maintain wealth.

3. "Rich People Are Greedy and Corrupt"

   - Origin: Stereotypes and media portrayals of wealthy individuals.
   - Impact: Creates a subconscious resistance to becoming wealthy and associating with wealthy people.

4. "I'll Never Be Able to Afford That"

   - Origin: Past financial struggles or a scarcity mindset.
   - Impact: Limits ambition and reduces efforts to improve financial circumstances.

5. "You Have to Work Hard to Make Money"

   - Origin: Cultural emphasis on hard work and traditional employment.
   - Impact: Overlooks opportunities for passive income, investments, and smarter financial strategies.

6. "There's Never Enough Money"

- Origin: Scarcity mindset and personal experiences of financial struggle.
- Impact: Promotes anxiety around finances and can lead to hoarding or excessive frugality.

7. "Talking About Money is Tacky or Impolite"

- Origin: Social norms and cultural taboos surrounding discussions of finances.
- Impact: Prevents open discussions about financial planning, investments, and learning from others' experiences.

8. "I'm Just Not Good with Money"

- Origin: Lack of financial education or past financial mistakes.
- Impact: Discourages learning about financial management and trying to improve financial literacy.

9. "Money Can't Buy Happiness"

- Origin: A common adage meant to highlight the value of non-material wealth.
- Impact: It can lead to neglecting financial health, even though financial stability contributes to overall well-being.

10. "I Should Save Every Penny"

- Origin: Fear of future financial instability or past experiences of lack.
- Impact: It can result in excessive frugality, preventing enjoyment of life and investments in personal growth.

Addressing and reframing these limiting beliefs through education, positive affirmations, and financial planning can help individuals develop healthier relationships with money and improve their financial situation.

IDENTIFYING LIMITING BELIEFS

Let's apply some critical thinking skills to our beliefs.

Take any one of the answers from the previous exercise and take them through the process below.

- Is it Provable?

- Is it Healthy?

- Is it Empowering?

- Is it Necessary?

- Is it Kind?

- Is it Loving?

- Is it Functional?

- Is it Rational?

- Is it Working?

- Do I want more of it?

- Does it feel Good?

TEN EMPOWERING BELIEF SHIFTS

1\. "I Must Be Perfect to Be Valued" → "I Know Who I Am"

- **Why It Works:** Embracing your true self removes the pressure to perform for external validation.
- **Action Step:** Write down three qualities about yourself that you love and share one with someone you trust.

2\. "Success Equals Happiness" → "My Happiness Creates My Success"

- **Why It Works:** Shifting the focus to joy allows success to flow naturally instead of being the ultimate goal.
- **Action Step:** Plan an activity today that (What activities) genuinely makes you happy, regardless of external outcomes.

3\. "It's Too Late to Change" → "My Decision to Change Can Happen in an Instant"

- **Why It Works:** Empowerment comes from realizing that transformation begins the moment you decide.
- **Action Step:** Choose one small habit to change today—something as simple as drinking more water or taking a walk. (One small action monthly)

4\. "I Am Not Enough" → "My Life Is a Gift to This Planet"

- **Why It Works:** This affirmation reconnects you with your unique value and purpose in the world.
- **Action Step:** Perform one act of kindness, no matter how small, to honor your role in the collective. (One small action monthly)

5. "I Must Conform to Fit In" → "I Am a Sovereign Being"

- **Why It Works:** Recognizing your autonomy fosters confidence and authenticity.
- **Action Step:** Make one decision today purely for yourself, without worrying about others' opinions. (One small decision monthly)

6. "Failure Is Unacceptable" → "My Last Lesson Prepared Me for the Next Journey"

- **Why It Works:** Viewing failure as a stepping stone removes fear and allows growth.
- **Action Step:** Reflect on a recent failure and list three things you learned from the experience. Make this reflection a habit.

7. "I Can't Ask for Help" → "It Is Okay to Be Vulnerable, and I Am Open to Support"

- **Why It Works:** Vulnerability strengthens connections and allows others to support you.
- **Action Step:** Reach out to someone for help or advice, even if it's as small as asking for a recommendation. Who can help you with what?

8. "I Should Have My Life Figured Out by Now" → "I Am Working Toward My Goals"

- **Why It Works:** Progress, not perfection, is the key to fulfillment.
- **Action Step:** Identify one small goal you can accomplish today and take a step toward it. (One small goal at a time; write your goals)

9. "I Don't Deserve Success" → "I Am Abundance, and I Embrace Opportunities When They Are Presented to Me"

- **Why It Works:** Affirming your worth opens the door to receiving abundance without guilt or hesitation.
- **Action Step:** Say "yes" to an opportunity that comes your way today, even if it feels intimidating.

10. "I Must Always Be Productive" → "When the Tide Is In, I Surf; When the Tide Is Out, I Watch the Sunset"

- **Why It Works:** This affirmation honors the natural ebb and flow of energy, promoting balance and self-care.
- **Action Step:** Schedule 15 minutes of intentional rest or relaxation today.

WHY EMPOWERING BELIEFS MATTER

Empowering beliefs do more than overwrite outdated, limiting ways of thinking; they help you **shift your focus from the problem space to the solution space**, encouraging action and growth without avoidance.

When you align your words, thoughts, and actions with these empowering beliefs, you create a ripple effect in your life. You're not just changing how you think; you're building a foundation for a life of purpose, joy, and success.

Actionable Steps

1 .- Identify one limiting belief you've been holding on to.

2 .- Choose an empowering belief from the list (or create your own) to replace it.

3 .- Speak it out loud and take one action today that reinforces this new belief.

**The journey to empowerment
begins with a single thought.
What belief will you choose to shift today?**

IF YOU WANT TO GO DEEPER

Transforming Through Soul Root Alchemy

Maybe you've already experienced a powerful shift during the course of this e-book or mini-course. Or perhaps you've stumbled upon something deeper—something bigger than what we've covered here—that you're ready to explore further.

Thoughts are powerful, but so are emotions. The mind is a gateway to the other realms of our inner world, including the emotions, the body, and the soul.

One of the most transformative tools we offer is something we call Soul Root Alchemy, which helps us unpack and discover our hidden underlying emotions and process them in a healthy way.

What Is Soul Root Alchemy?

Soul Root Alchemy is a systematic approach to unpacking the limiting beliefs, old stories, upsets, traumas, and triggers that hold us back. By examining these pieces of our past, we learn to see them for what they truly are—opportunities for growth and transformation.

But this isn't just about reframing thoughts or addressing mental constructs. Soul Root Alchemy goes deeper into the emotions that keep those limiting beliefs alive.

How Does It Work?

- Unpacking the Story: We examine the narratives we tell ourselves and identify the limiting beliefs tied to them.
- Transmuting the Emotions: By working through the emotions surrounding these stories, we change the way we relate to them.
- Rewriting the Narrative: Once the emotional charge is dissolved, the story itself transforms. With it, we can create new, healthier, and more functional beliefs.

When we release the emotional weight of the past, it no longer controls us. We reclaim our power to consciously write a new story, one rooted in growth, resilience, and self-love.

Turning Lead Into Gold

In the simplest terms, Soul Root Alchemy is about transformation—turning the "lead" of limiting beliefs into the "gold" of empowerment and possibility. This isn't just a metaphor; it's a practice. It's the process of finding the hidden gift in every challenge and using it to fuel your rapid growth. If you're ready to delve deeper into this powerful process, remember the transformation begins with your willingness **to face the old and let it go. What new story will you write today?**

This marks the conclusion of Book 1 (of 4) in "A Grand Path" series.

This journey wasn't about learning, it was about "un-learning". It's about shedding the weight that holds us down and breaking the chains that prevent us from embracing our true, naturally extraordinary selves.

For some, this book has served as a simple refresher course; for others, it's been a coaching tool. Some may find it to be their first step into the realm of shadow work, uncovering the unseen aspects of them-selves they have yet to meet. Regardless of where you are on your journey, I challenge you to regularly question every belief you hold. The falsehoods will crumble, leaving only what truly matters.

While we've only scratched the surface of the mental realm, my hope is that this book has provided valuable insights and supported your progress in breaking the spells that bind you.

In Book 2, we'll venture into the emotional realm, exploring the deep-rooted beliefs that stubbornly resist release. Together, we'll uncover and transform the energetic charge beneath those layers.

If you have questions, would like to offer feedback, or are looking for continued support on your journey regarding this book series, please request to join my private Facebook group:

https://www.facebook.com/groups/grandpath

Be a part of the community and a contributor to future publishings!

9 798896 912071